SENTIMENTAL
B L U E

T0294290

SENTIMENTAL
BLUE

Jefferson Carter

chax

2007

Cover painting: *Olla*, by Jim Waid (acrylic on canvas, 1997)

ISBN 978-0-925904-62-1

Grateful acknowledgment is made to the following publications in which
some of these poems first appeared, often in slightly different forms.

> *Barrow Street,* "The Sanctificationist of Ajo"
>
> *The Missing Fez,* "Starry Night"
>
> *Poets Against the War,* "Civilians"
>
> *Tucson Guide,* "A Centaur"
>
> *2River View,* "The Avant-Garde," "The Mummy"

For Connie and for Evan . . . always

CONTENTS

A CENTAUR

For laughs,
I imitate a horse,
lowering my bare shoulder
into the sand
of the arroyo, my wife
watching from above
& our son inside the blue backpack
watching while I roll, kicking
my hooves & neighing, husband
turned centaur, father
as some big animal.
The boy laughs
because his mother's laughing
& I lurch to my feet, shaking,
blowing through my nostrils,
feeling foolish,
but what's a family for?
Climbing back up,
I smell creosote & sage
& I understand the Greeks
who carried in their armor
a bag of spices
that smelled like home.

STREP THROAT

I sleep in my son's bed,
his comforter billowing
over me like meringue,
the poems of Che Guevara
under my pillow.
When my wife comes home,
she lets the dog in,
the dog who loves me
unconditionally. What did
Che call his apolitical friends?
Drunks, singing, their throats
about to be cut. The dog
loves me for myself, morose,
apolitical, the tang of penicillin
on my skin & he scuttles
down the hall, wondering
where I am, finally
wriggling the comforter
aside & draping himself
over my head like
someone's flung beret.

ELAVIL

Every family has that story
about grandpa getting blue
& going to bed for a month,
curtains drawn. When I get blue
it's no joke. Ask a Mormon
missionary how he feels,
bugging housewives, wiping
spit off his shoes. Elavil
online, one-hundred dollars
for thirty caps. Possible side effects—
black tongue, breast development
in males, coma, hives,
strange taste, swollen testicles,
stroke, vomiting, red
or purple spots on skin.
How low can you go? How high
can you get? Me? When I'm happy
I sign all my e-mails XOXOXO.

STARRY NIGHT

We went to Dee's for dinner
& I got into her medicine cabinet.
I floated through dessert
like a starry night. My internist,
a good guy, really, but he wears
these beads & tells stupid jokes.
I kept dropping hints—
I pee all night. I break things.
I forgot a jacket somewhere.
Would Valium help? Or
something stronger?   He acts
like I'm Van Gogh waving
a butter knife. Remember
Joni Mitchell? How she
kidded around? Hey, man,
do "Starry Night" again, man.

BIPOLAR

I'd rather be William Blake than
Tommy Hilfiger. If I could practice
yoga 22/7, I'd be fine. Acupuncture
five hours a day & I'd be better.
My dad used to say, before he
got into trouble, stay in bed & stay
out of trouble. All my son's friends
could start an alt-rock big band called
The Bipolar Bears. Can you empathize?
Look in a mirror & see nothing but
the back of your head? O.K. Let's
lighten up. How about a glam-country
band called Tommy & The Duster Bunnies?

CHARLES FISHMAN KICKS ME
OUT OF HIS READING

The drug helps me see
the half-full glass. People
really are "interesting."
When I listen to the President
my nausea's not so bad.
A wound's been reciting
its poetry & I wish I'd upped
my dose. My yoga teacher says
tune into your inner body.
My inner body huddles, hands
over its ears, sitz bones rattling
this plastic seat. My outer body
turns to the woman beside me
& hums "We gotta get outta this place,"
loud enough for the wound
to hear.
        Rain's drenched the hedges,
which smell like mint. Unbelievable–
kicked out of a poetry reading!
I remember a line from a movie, "Hey,
let's go watch them slaughter
the sheep." Did you know
sheep sneeze when they're afraid?
Now that, that sounds like fun.

THE AVANT-GARDE

My son's legs hurt,
he can't hike or horse around.
He sits in front of the tv, icing
his knees & playing video games.
Here I'd like to admit
the personal lyric is dead,
the lie of the unitary self,
the poet as sensitive register.
Signifiers hit the window
like birds, smearing the glass.
Yes, the personal lyric is dead
but life goes on, ignoring
the avant-garde, the head games
& bad puns. Anyway, back
to the bourgeois subject,
my son's legs, which hurt
while he directs the wobbly,
red-caped character that signifies
himself acting in the world, this
character that runs everywhere
instead of walking.

VANITY WESTERN

How not to write
a sex scene: "Next
came her bloomers.
She stood before him, a
fully naked adult woman.
They both got into the bedroll
for a night of sexual
satisfaction to both parties."

Go ahead. Laugh.
Here's his disclaimer:
"The author intends no
harm or injury to anyone."

He wants me to edit
his next western. I just might.
I'd correct his punctuation
but edit all that inchoate
love? No way.

He sent me a photo
of the winner's circle,
his scruffy bay colt, his
daughters beaming & there,
behind the grandchildren,
someone he just met, me.
His wife on one side, him
on the other, their arms
around my waist.

WRITING IN THE SHOWER

I wanted something
Eastern European, you know,
something portentous
in the best sense of the word,
but what I managed was
two lines of Southwestern
animal husbandry, half
a simile comparing
something wet to a teaser
stallion on a stud farm
& I was too busy
to mention the sow bugs
in the shower stall,
which echoed like a school
for famous writers.

LAND OF THE PHARAOHS

I like being called "brother"
by black men. I like walking past
Land of the Pharaohs
& being invited in by the brothers
to bless them with a poem.
"Brothers," I say, "brothers,
please, no keyboards, no congas,
let me lay something white & uptight
on you brothers." I recite my poem
about Martians & Geiger counters,
its conclusion an ironic invitation
to Jesus to drop by some morning
for coffee. They hate it.
The brothers hate it
but they're polite, not like Kerouac
at the Living Theater
heckling Frank O'Hara
or the Academy Awards audience
mocking poor Sally Fields
when she said "You
like me! You really do
like me!" The brothers forgive me
as they'd forgive a flying nun
who alighted among them
& roosted, preening, while a brother
recited his hip-hop poem called
"Kill the White Muthafuckers."

THE SANCTIFICATIONIST OF AJO

Founder & ramrod, a proponent
of least said is soonest mended,
she bermed the soil, certain
the workings of the spirit transform us
into raised flower beds,
her sanctification a thorn in the flesh
of those husbands subject to root rot
& a face-saving semblance
of daytime control. Oh, that shadow war
on rooftops, every woman beholden
for small necessities, every man
an unflappable giant, striding
as if he owned the town.

EXEMPLAR

I can't believe I'm telling my son
about the good old days, my travels
& sexual conquests. He pretends
he's not listening, then says that's disgusting.
I agree. Staying with Cornelia in Augsburg,
visiting her family, her mother who didn't
understand why the Allies bombed Munich,
the horizon burning, her father, a one-legged
shadow who escaped through his study window
when company knocked. I wasn't company,
more like a plague visited upon them, eating
their food, speaking English, fucking their daughter
every night in her childhood bed, doggy-style,
staring at the mandala between my thumbs,
sometimes thinking take that & that & that
because it felt so good & because no one
ever mentioned Nazis or the Jews. Better
left unsaid, these stories, these examples
I set for my son, who keeps saying
that's disgusting, that's so disgusting.

CIVILIANS

for John Crow

Nobody wants the Osama bin Bush
T-shirts. I can't even give away
the Ashamed To Be American trucker caps.
The al-Qaida Hearts My Gas Hog
bumper stickers? Another flop.
I have to sneak around at night
& superglue them to the neighbors' SUVs.
Officially, the invasion killed 1500 civilians,
give or take 500. The woman I approach
outside Safeway says that's ok. She's wearing
her sequined Bring 'em On bustier
& her Uncle Sam's Got Balls jester cap.
Yes, she's sure she doesn't want some God
Forgive America hard hats for the kids.

DUMBFUCKISTAN

We've been following this chick band
since London, where Teddy, who can't get
laid, skinny-dipped in the flooded roundabout,
two older chicks breast-stroking
nearby & looking, as the song goes,
for adventure. Teddy's such a tool!
He forgot to laugh at himself & blew
his one good line. You touch your tattoo
of Old Glory & say you're from Dumbfuckistan,
usually you hook up. On stage, Y's wearing
those lame suede shorts & over her head
a paper bag decorated with the photo
of a missing child. X & Z, sharing a pair of
three-legged leather pants, spank tambourines
against their middle leg. Oh well, as I keep
telling Teddy, anything's better than living in
Dumbfuckistan, back, as the song says,
in the U.S. of A. I guess it's hokey-pokey time.
The word? The boys from Dumbfuckistan
will do anything. Teddy's in the front row,
yelling that joke someone told him, "What's got
two thumbs & eats pussy? This guy!"

POEMHUNTER.COM

I look in the mirror.
I like what I see.

Not really. Some singer
wrote those words.

Gladys M. e-mails me
from St. Paul: I like

your poem. I'm 14.
How old are you?

My wife tells me don't
reply. What? My one fan

& she's FBI? Is sex
the new sex?

Hey, writes Cherry Gee,
13, from Sioux Falls, so

what else is new?

MUSIC MIX

The song begins "Don't go
like a lamb to slaughter.
I'll haul the wood. I'll carry
water." I don't know
if it's a protest song
or a love song. When "rain"
rhymes with "mountain"
I know it's a love song.
My love song would go like this:
"I love the small of your back.
I love the large of your back."
You're so crazy. You walk
down the street of logos.
Is that Bruce Willis over there
or your therapist? It's all good
even when it's not. It's all
good even when it's not.

BAD GIRL

Why wouldn't you
fuck me? I used to be
bad too. Dealt cocaine.
Went down on
someone going down
on someone else
in a car parked outside
a night club. OK,
that word "dealt"
isn't exactly street.
I'm overeducated, I
admit it, quoting Byron
about passion, "the sword
outwears its sheath"
& Pater, how we must "burn
always with a hard,
gem-like flame."
I'm married. So what?
I can burn that way.
You're too old for those

combat boots & tattoos,
the razor wire around
your wrists & down
your spine, those strangers
saying "Man, she's
wild." You noticed
my biceps, more gristle
than muscle. I know
you saw the skull shining
beneath my pompadour.
So what? You didn't even
give me the chance to
turn you down.

TWITCH

She says you're doing that
thing again & nods at the fork
jiggling in my hand. Parkinson's?
Multiple sclerosis? Nerve cancer?
I don't want to know. How can I
stop this twitching? Stare hard
at my hand. Poor raccoon,
don't wash your food. I know
she loves me. She says
now you're doing that other thing.

MY FIRST LOVE

You bitched about my kisses,
too tentative, like one
of those toy birds dipping
its beak into a glass of water.
You're coming to visit me
& my wife. Who wants to hear
Etta sing "The Jealous Kind"?
I used sex to stay on top.
Once I compared
an old lover's nipples
to tiny sombreros & you
looked at me with such pity
I felt myself disappear.

FINALLY, A LOVE POEM
FOR MY WIFE

You're my sticky mat, my
power anthem, my vertebrae
like pearls on a string,
one at a time. You read me
letters to the editor, news
from the parallel universe:
"Simply look at the man
who is our president, see
a good man, with a good heart."
You tell me funny stories,
someone's son explaining he
can't watch gratuitous violence
but he can watch historical
violence. Or some kid defining
the parts of speech: Lungs. Air.
You're my lungs, my air.

THUNDER

Lightning, then, of course, thunder.
We can get used to anything.
The window, lit up, shakes
& we're comforted, pulling
the blankets to our chins. The dog,
half-blind, diabetic, fat as a woodchuck,
burrows between us, panting,
trembling like she's never heard
thunder before. Maybe she hasn't,
she lives so much in the moment.
Here's her day: I was in. Now I'm out.
I was out. Now I'm in. You going
to eat that? You going to eat that?
I'll eat that! Here's her night so far:
What's that? Thunder. What's that?
Thunder. What's that? Thunder.

LITTER BOX

My wife asked me this morning
if I'd ever cheated on her.
My ex-wife called this afternoon
& asked me the same thing.
What's going on?
That new Italian movie
the art film crowd adores,
the characters hysterical, nearly
operatic, their marriages dead
or dying. I imagine all the couples
sipping cappuccino after the movie,
nibbling biscotti, that close
to confessing their own infidelities.
I love my wife. I don't whine
about my latest chore, cleaning
the litter box four or five times
a day. I can imagine one
of those histrionic Italian husbands
fuming, yearning for his mistress
as he kneels by the reeking box,

scooping cat feces & urinous clots
of litter into a plastic bag.
The second I'm done, our old cat
comes running. Otherwise,
he limps from room to room, moaning
like the ghost of some animal
whose bladder burst.
I love that old cat. Most nights
he snuggles under the comforter,
buzzing between me & my wife like a
space heater I need to repair.

THE MINOTAUR

Am I impressed? I suppose.
The bull's head, the horns,
the way you puff up
three times your size. Still
you're the same old, same old.
Considerate. A bit of a slob.
Some drool, green as mint,
on your side of the pillow.

THE FIRST SALTIST CHURCH
OF TARIQ OUR LORD

Whenever my mother mentions
Jesus, I praise Tariq, how,
2000 years ago, his spaceship
crash landed in central Utah.
Tariq, the Prince of Saltus, Tariq,
the 10-foot-tall alien who talks to me
in my dreams, whose ship of salt
dissolved in the 100-year rain.
I pray twice a day, facing
the Great Salt Lake. I drink a glass
of salt water each night.
When this world of tears ends,
when Lord Tariq returns, the planet
Saltus blood-red on the horizon,
the faithful will be like unto salt crystals,
the sweat drying on his awful brow.
My proof? Look at our language.
"Salt of the earth," "salty dog,"
"the unplumbed, salt, estranging sea."
And tell me this: when it
rains, what pours?

NEGATIVE

You shake her hand—
like crushing an onion skin
she's so enlightened.
I used to call her parents
Old Negative & Old Positive.
One possessed an immortal soul,
the other didn't. They both
drank themselves to death.
Nikhal, 14, e-mails
her from Malaysia:
"our soul from heaven,
is sacred, we can't pollude
it with immoral word."
Ain't that the fuckin' truth!
She's practicing non-attachment
to this world of illusion,
given away her favorite books,
that copy of *Reservation Blues*,
the one inscribed to her:
"If you were an Apple,
I'd still love you. Best,

Sherman Alexie."
I call the ashram
but she's busy. I leave
a message Old Negative
would have loved: "Any
of you guys want a brewski?
Tell me what's Sanskrit
for six pack & I'll buy."

PRETTY

Our sensei tells us the body's a wave
in an ocean of energy, an endlessly reborn wave.
Hemingway, about to eat his shotgun, thought
it would be pretty to think so. Yes, it would.
Our cat comes skidding into the bathroom
whenever I use the electric toothbrush.
She must think I'm purring. Any other
sound & she freaks. When I'm in bed
reading another novel about cancer, somebody
suffering, the cat's nowhere to be found.
I could use the comfort. The gauze unwound,
the staples removed, these bruises really do
resemble the fanciest shades of paint, Hyacinth,
Barn, Folksy Gold, Sentimental Blue.

THE MUMMY

Wrapped in my blue & white striped
100% Egyptian cotton bed sheet
I skulk in the vestibule. What a word—
ves.ti.bule, the last syllable
like breathing on a mirror. I overheard
two girls laughing about their teacher
arrested taking out the garbage
in his underwear. I say more power
to him. I'll say to those girls the night
I catch them, have a little mercy.
Mercy, a word that sounds
like someone swallowing flowers.

WHAT I DID IN HEAVEN

Flapped around. Practiced
safe sex. Egg white
instead of semen.

Yoga was the best,
the clouds breathing us,
every pose perfected,

I even did Vanquished Warrior,
that *asana* most women
on earth can do.

Can I come back now?

ABOUT THE AUTHOR

Jefferson Carter has lived in Tucson, Arizona, since 1954. A writing instructor at Pima Community College, the Downtown Campus, he teaches developmental composition and poetry writing. Currently, he is the Writing Department Chair.

He has won a Tucson/Pima Arts Council Literary Arts Fellowship, and his poems have appeared in such journals and e-zines as *Carolina Quarterly, CrossConnect, 2River View*, and *Barrow Street*. His chapbook *Tough Love* won the Riverstone Poetry Press Award.

This is his seventh book of poetry.

Also from Chax Press

Glen Mott, *Analects*
Bruce Andrews, *Swoon Noir*
Charles Borkhuis, *Afterimage*
Joe Amato, *Under Virga*
David Abel, *Black Valentine*
Paul Naylor, *Arranging Nature*
Kass Fleisher, *Accidental Species*
Tenney Nathanson, *Erased Art*
Heather Nagami, *Hostile*
Linh Dinh, *American Tatts*
Patrick Pritchett, *Burn: Doxology for Joan of Arc*
Jonathan Brannen, *Deaccessioned Landscapes*
Beverly Dahlen, *A-Reading Spicer & 18 Sonnets*
Elizabeth Treadwell, *Chantry*

For our many additional titles please visit our web site:
http://www.chax.org/

Chax Press is supported by the Tucson Pima Arts Council
and by the Arizona Commission on the Arts with funding
from the State of Arizona and the National Endowment
for the Arts.